XTREME ILLUSIONS

LOOK . . . AND LOOK AGAIN

THE DIZZY ZONE

THE GRAND TOUR OF CRAZY PLACES
PAGE **38**

LOOPY LINES AND SILLY SIZES

PAGE **30**

NATIONAL GEOGRAPHIC

WASHINGTON, D.C.

WARNING!

YOU ARE NOW ENTERING

THE DIZZY ZONE

HOLD ON TIGHT FOR THE NEXT FEW PAGES.

There are illusions to scramble your eyeballs, boggle your brain, and turn your knees to jelly.

5

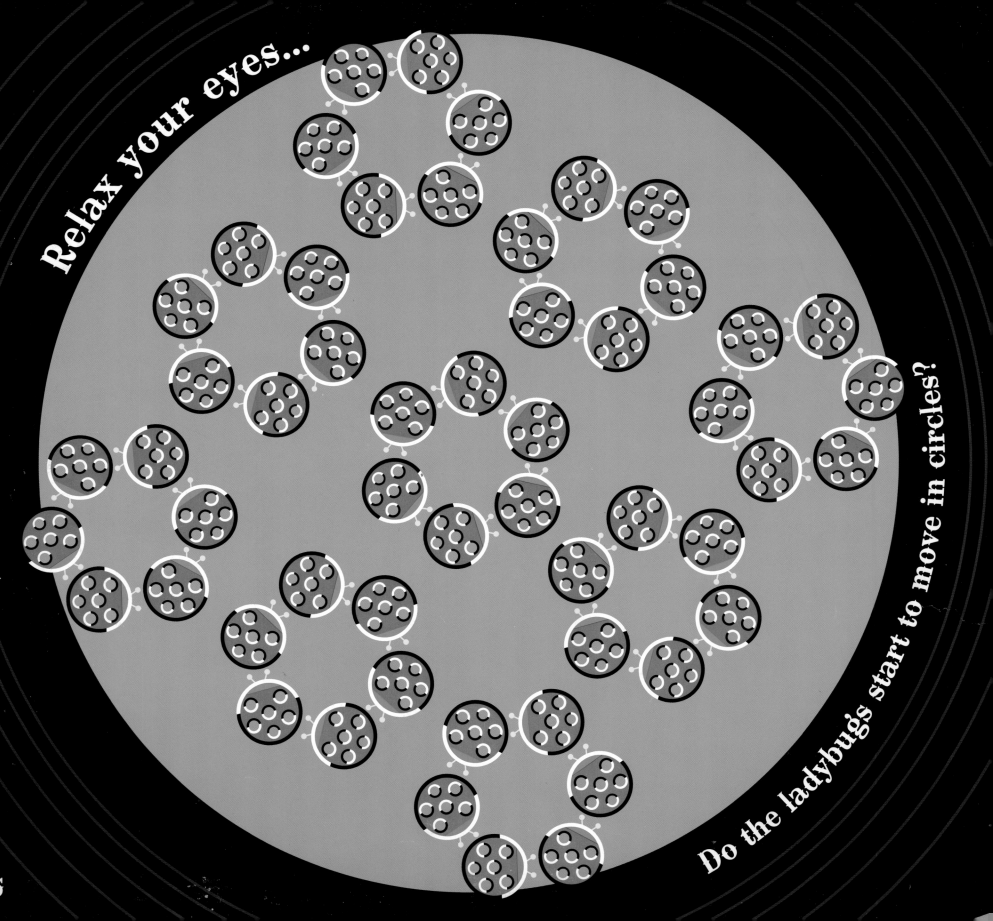

Do the ladybugs start to move in circles?

6

WATCH
AS THIS NEST OF **SNAKES** BEGINS TO UNCOIL...

Each "snake" is a set of smaller and smaller rings, whose color patterns do not line up. But your brain likes to keep things simple and orderly, so it tries to match up the same colors by "twisting" the rings in your mind, making them appear to turn.

MOVE YOUR EYES AROUND THIS GRID AND WATCH AS THE DOTS CHANGE FROM GRAY TO WHITE TO GRAY AGAIN.

Looking at one spot shows that it's white. But when you look slightly to the side, your brain saves time and effort by guessing that the gray nes continue through the spot, so the spot looks gray too.

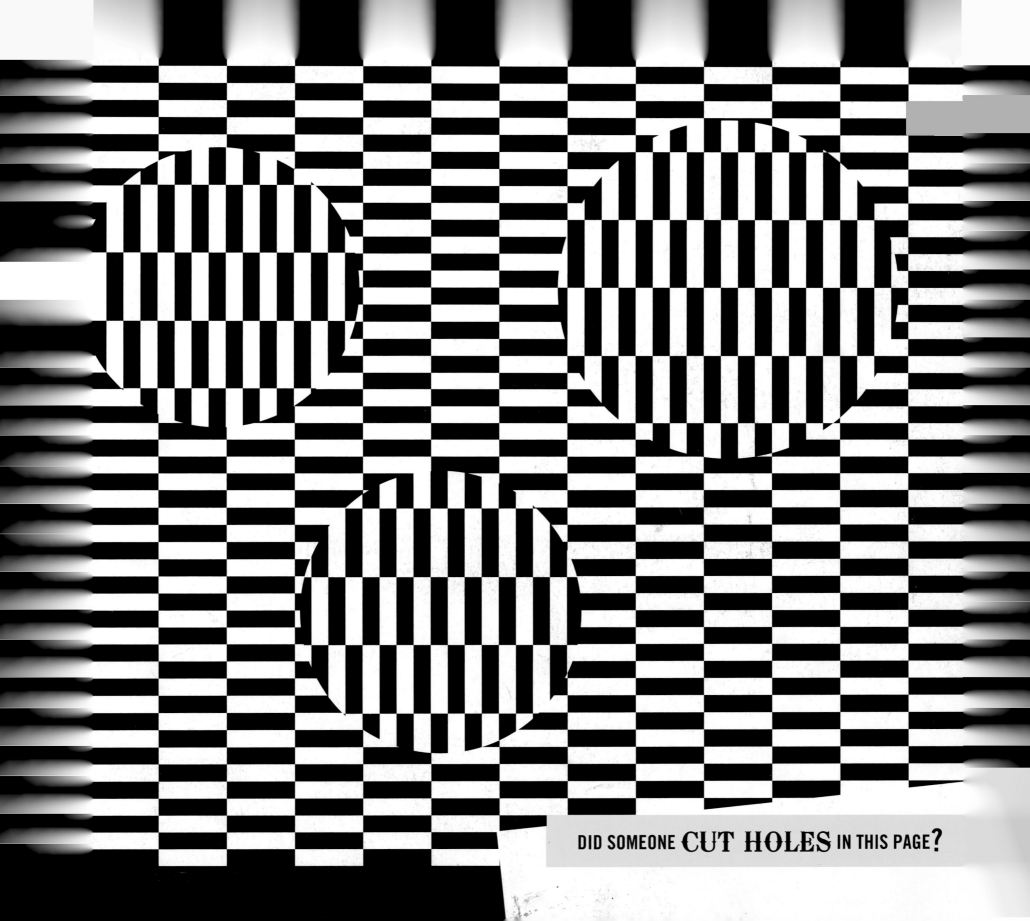

DID SOMEONE **CUT HOLES** IN THIS PAGE?

HEY!

Who stretched the page?

On a round object, like a ball, the parts of any surface pattern look thinner as they curve away. This effect, where more distant things look smaller, is called perspective, and the flat pattern here illustrates it.

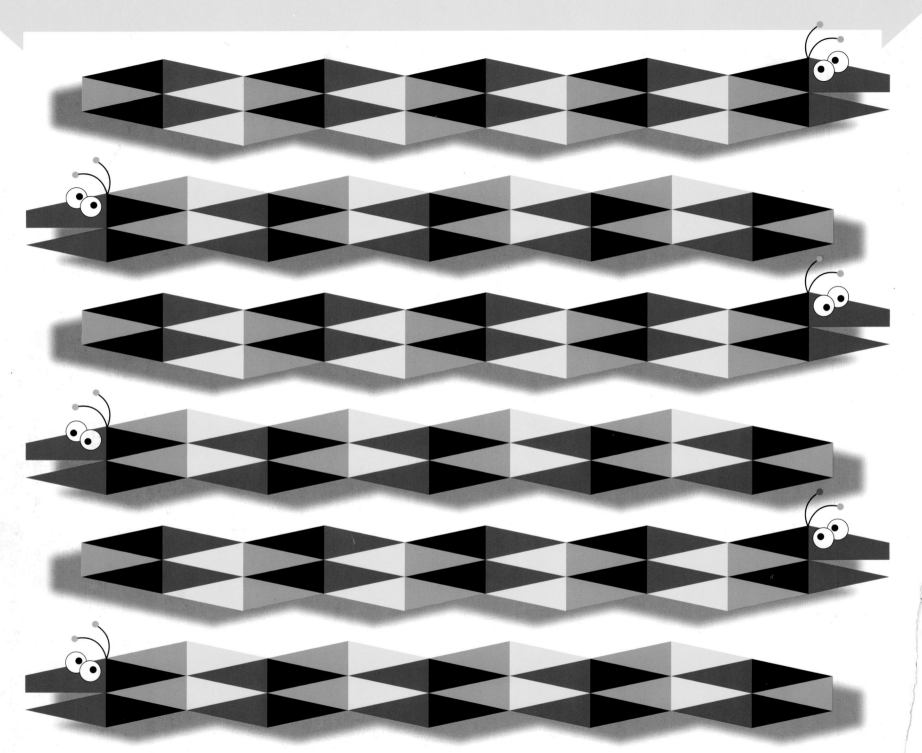

The caterpillars are not stacked perfectly, one above the other. But your brain wants them to look neat, so it makes the caterpillars "creep" into line. The effect is increased by the shadows, which point away from the caterpillars' heads.

FEELING DIZZY YET?

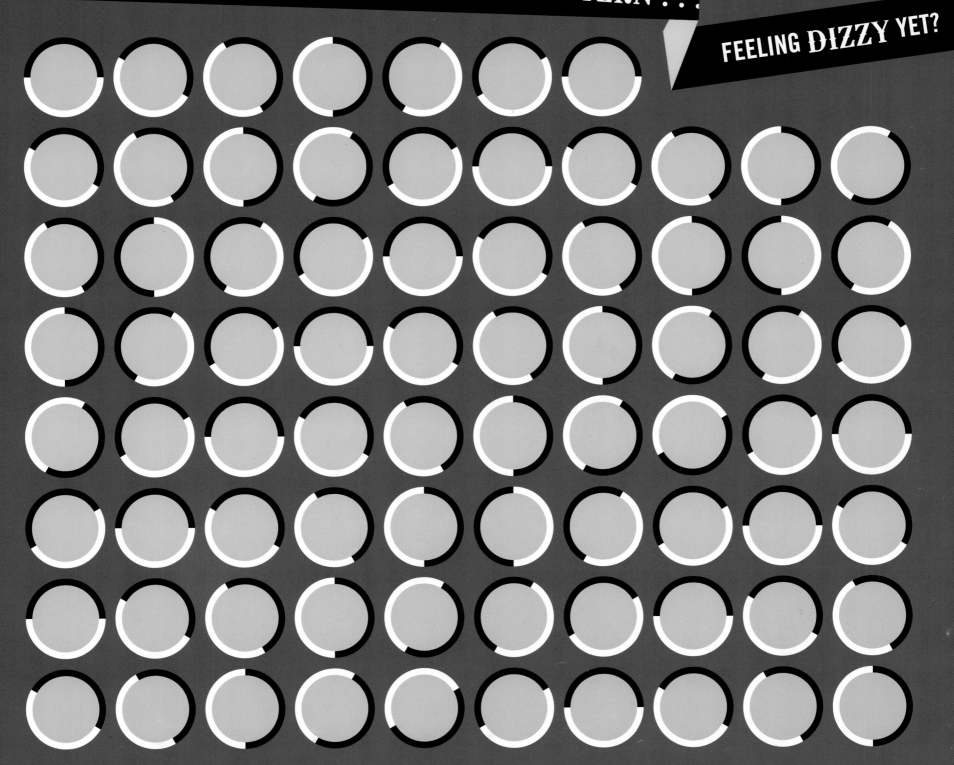

13

HERE'S AN ILLUSION THAT'S SURE TO
MAKE YOUR EYES POP OUT!

14

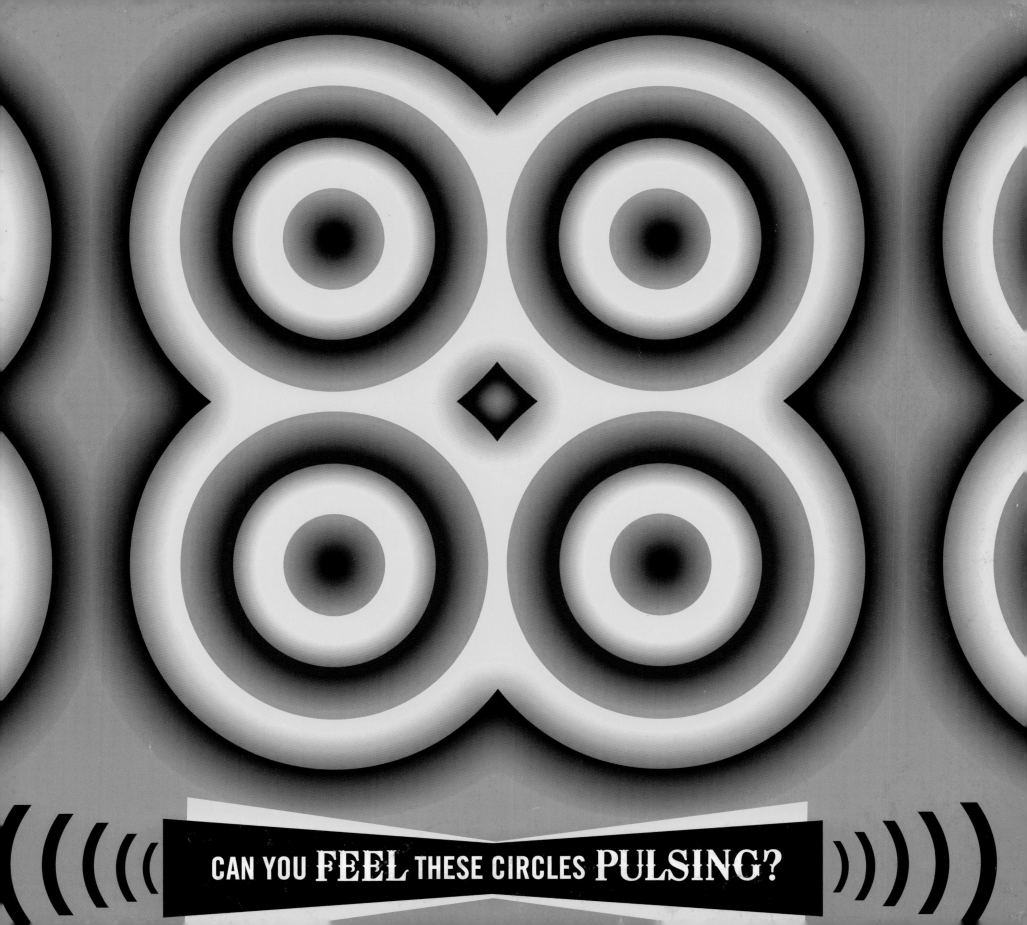

CAN YOU **FEEL** THESE CIRCLES **PULSING?**

LOOK

...and look again!

NOTHING IS QUITE AS IT SEEMS ON THE FOLLOWING PAGES. Look for impossible objects, hidden secrets, and doorways to incredible worlds.

Are you looking at a painting of a view from a window or the actual view? Artist René Magritte (1898-1967) painted common objects and familiar scenes, but combined them in unusual ways.

17

Plenty to drink
but not a glass in sight **?**

OR

rows of glasses
with nothing to fill them **?**

What a beautiful display of fruit!

BUT CAN YOU FIND TWO HUNGRY PEOPLE **?** READY TO START EATING

The brain quickly sees the bright, colorful fruit. Then it notices the two white faces created by the outline of the fruit. Your brain "flips" between the two views. This is called a figure-ground illusion: The fruit is the figure (the main object), and the faces are the ground (background).

HOW WILL THE COACHMAN CROSS THE BROKEN BRIDGE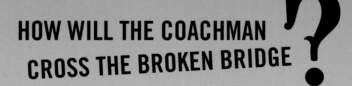

Stare at the damaged part of the bridge and relax your eyes,
as if you are looking right through the page.

The bridge will be repaired as if by magic!

IS THIS PERSON HAPPY OR SAD ?

We are so used to seeing faces, we "force" the lines in this picture into facial features, but they change depending on which way is up. The happy forehead wrinkle becomes an unhappy mouth, and the raised eyebrows turn into sad lines under the eyes, and so on.

Turn the page upside down.

Turn the page upside down.

DO YOU SEE **LAZY** ELEPHANTS?

OR **LEAPING** ELEPHANTS?

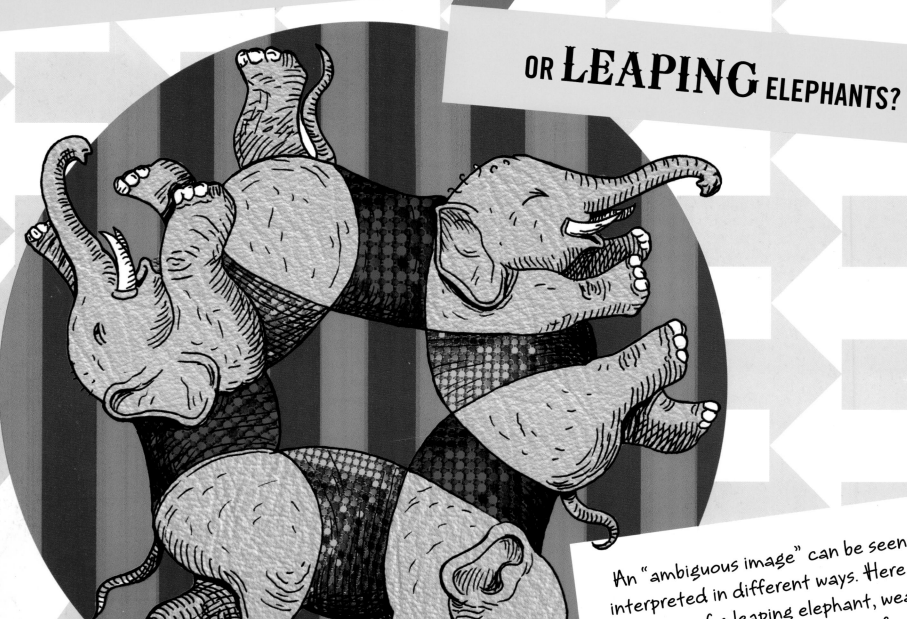

An "ambiguous image" can be seen or interpreted in different ways. Here the back legs of a leaping elephant, wearing purple, are also the back legs of a lazy elephant, wearing gold. Your brain cannot decide which set of elephants the legs belong to.

THE CHESHIRE CAT SAYS THAT THE ARROWS WILL HELP ALICE FIND HER WAY.

BUT SHOULD SHE CHOOSE THE BLUE ONES OR THE WHITE ONES?

DOES THIS PERSON LOOK **STRANGE** OR **NORMAL** PERFECTLY **?**

(*Now turn the page upside down.*)

24

WHAT DO YOU SEE ?

Billowing smoke from a fire on the hill....
or the flowing hair of a beautiful girl?

Tilt the page to read the secret message below.

NOW TILT THE PICTURE OPPOSITE

AND LOOK IN THE DIRECTION OF THE

ARROW TO FIND THE HIDDEN SKULL.

This odd station entrance is really just a big drawing! The steps, railings, White Rabbit, and Alice and other people have so much detail that they look three-dimensional. In fact they are drawn on a sidewalk and the wall behind!

LOOK CLOSER...

COULD YOU REALLY WALK DOWN THESE STEPS?

AND IS THIS PERSON REALLY ABOUT TO BE EATEN FOR DINNER?

LOOPY LINES & SILLY SIZES

THE NEXT ROUND OF ILLUSIONS IS ABOUT SIZE, SHAPE, AND DIRECTION.

If you suspect your eyes are playing tricks on you, grab this ruler and put the illusions to the test!

Is this really a spiral? Trace one of the curved lines with your finger and decide for yourself!

ARE THE LONGER LINES PARALLEL TO EACH OTHER ?

Use your ruler to find out!

Here the short lines create a background that distorts the long parallel lines. Because the short lines are at an angle, they make one end of each long line seem closer than the other. The switching angle of the short lines makes the long lines appear to pull in opposite directions.

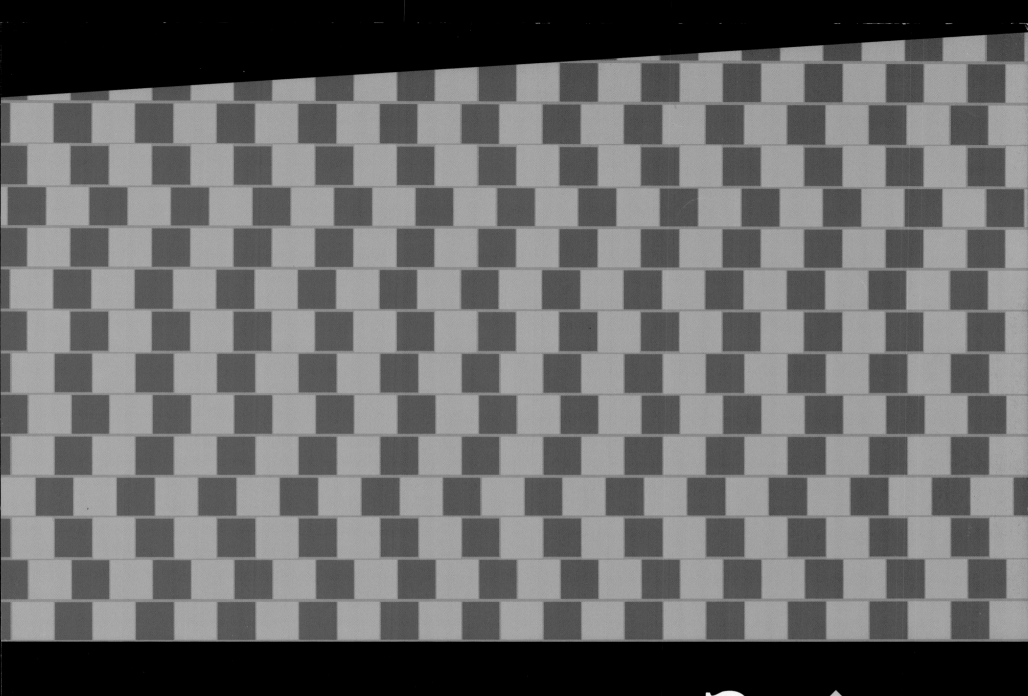

WHAT ABOUT THESE HORIZONTAL STRIPES?

Are they parallel or do they slant?

TWO PRETTY FLOWERS—BUT WHICH HAS THE **BIGGEST** ORANGE CENTER?

When things are close together, we are good at comparing their sizes. Here the left flower's little petals make its center look big, while the right flower's large petals make its center seem small. But the two centers are far apart, so the brain does not realize that they are the same size.

Lines coming together show perspective and seem to stretch into the distance. The topmost banana is near where the lines meet, so the brain thinks it's the farthest away. Yet, because it looks the same size as the other bananas, we assume it's the biggest, too.

THIS MONKEY WANTS THE
BIGGEST BANANA HE CAN FIND.

WHICH ONE SHOULD HE CHOOSE?

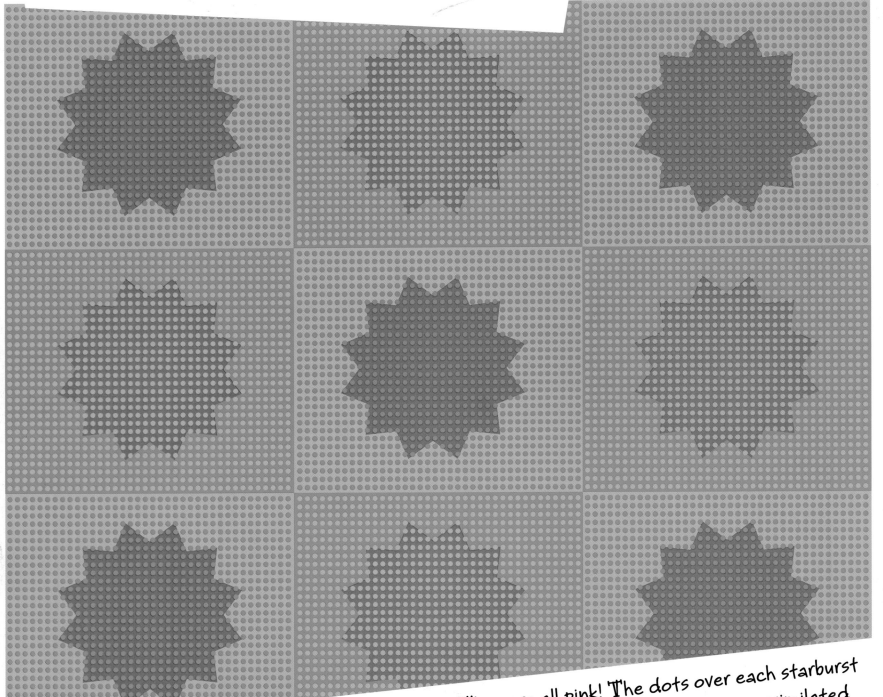

They are neither. They are all pink! The dots over each starburst make us see it in a color that is more similar to, or assimilated into, its own. The differing color of the background heightens the effect, known as color assimilation and contrast.

PATTERN SEEMS EXTREMELY WOBBLY AT THE CENTER.

Use your ruler to see if this is really the case.

THE GRAND TOUR OF CRAZY PLACES

ARE YOUR EYES SCRAMBLED ENOUGH?

If not, then join this tour of the most crazy places imaginable. Could they really exist?

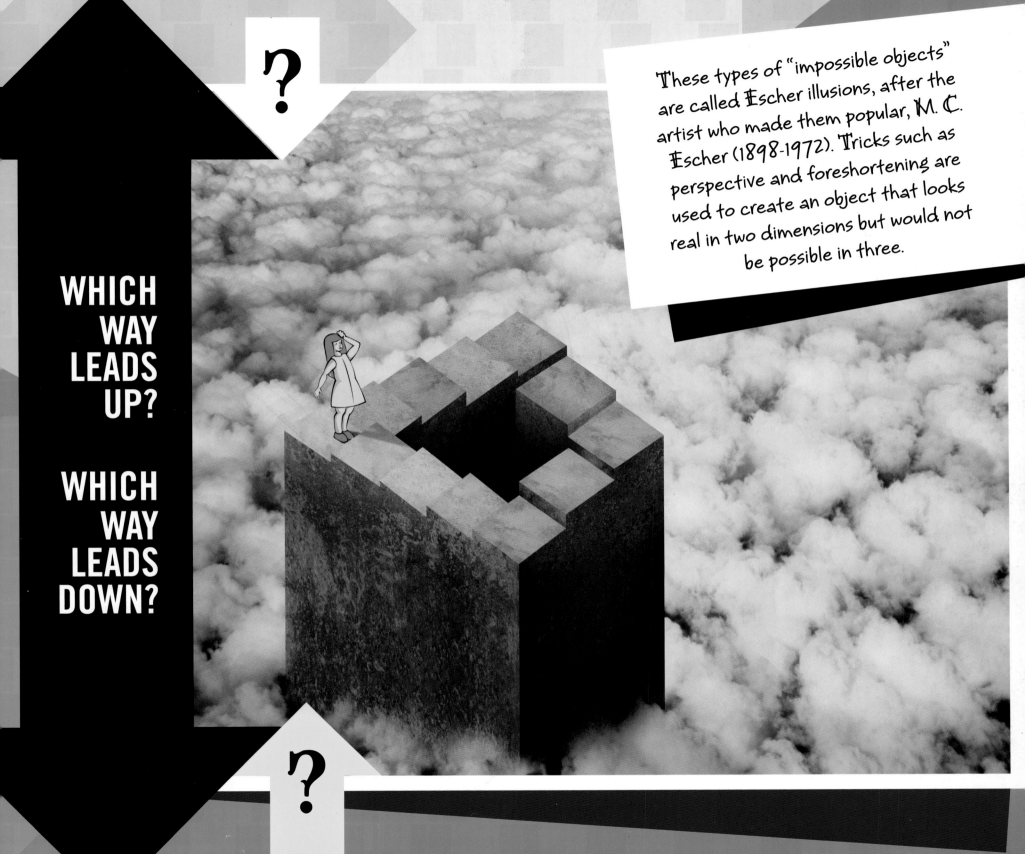

WHICH
WAY
LEADS
UP?

WHICH
WAY
LEADS
DOWN?

These types of "impossible objects" are called Escher illusions, after the artist who made them popular, M. C. Escher (1898-1972). Tricks such as perspective and foreshortening are used to create an object that looks real in two dimensions but would not be possible in three.

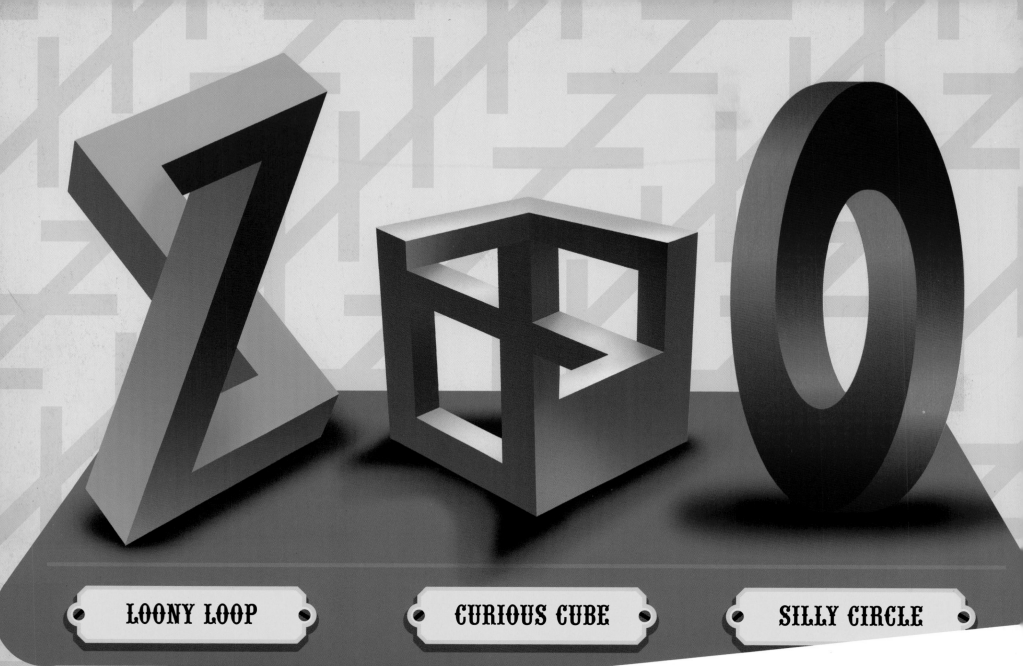

LOONY LOOP

CURIOUS CUBE

SILLY CIRCLE

Could ANY of the exhibits in the **Museum of Wonders** really exist **?**

The truth is that none of these curious objects are possible. While they might look solid enough, the edges and surfaces combine in a way that simply couldn't occur. Try following an edge with your finger as if you were touching a real object - you'll soon find it to be **very strange indeed!**

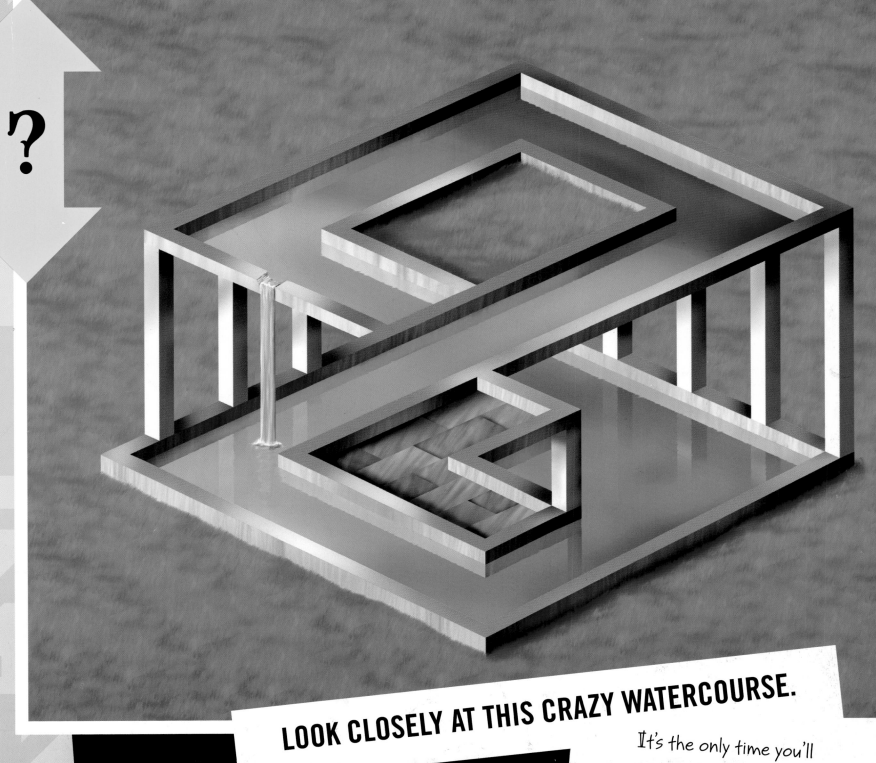

?

LOOK CLOSELY AT THIS CRAZY WATERCOURSE.

It's the only time you'll see water flow uphill!

CAN YOU DETECT ANYTHING STRANGE ABOUT THESE STEPS

A CLUE: look closely at the gray bar halfway up the staircase...

In paradox illusions, features seem to oppose or go against each other—they are "paradoxical." Under the chimney, the wall's angle suggests that its left side sits farther back than its right side. But at the lower left, the part that sticks out makes the left side appear to be in front of the right.

43

How can three chimney openings have four bases? Look at the crane's load too! Long parallel lines are joined and shaded at one end to suggest one set of three-dimensional objects, but another set at the other end.

On the right, the windows and steps give the impression of walls and flat floors. Follow the horizontal lines left, and the walls become floors, while the floors turn into walls. This illusion works best with a slight "gap" in the middle of each level, with just horizontal lines and no other details.

Carlton Books
Publisher – Sam Sweeney
Creative Director – Clare Baggaley
Senior Editor – Anna Bowles
Executive Editor – Barry Timms
Consultant – Steve Parker
Art Editor – Emily Clarke
Designer – Ceri Woods
Picture Research – Ben White
Production – Christine Ni

Published by the National Geographic Society, Washington, D.C. 20036.

Text, design, and illustration
© Carlton Books Limited 2012

Trade ISBN: 978-1-4263-1011-9
Reinforced library editon ISBN: 978-1-4263-1084-3

Printed in Dongguan, China
12 / CAR / 2

Picture Credits